Reflections Thru My Windshield

Part 3

Dave Madill

Reflections Thru My Windshield
Part 3
Copyright © 2008 by David R. Madill

A **Write Up The Road** Book

For more information contact:
Write Up The Road Publishing
P.O. Box 69
Kenton, TN 38233
(800) 292-8072
www.writeuptheroad.com

Reflections Thru My Windshield   Part 3
Madill, David R.
ISBN: 09766872-8-3

Cover design by Timothy D. Brady
Printed in the United States of America

Memories and Echoes

What brings on these words and causes me to write

Why do dreams and memories chase me thru the night

Tales of fact and fancy and senseless little rhymes

Why do they run thru my head and lodge in the crevices
of my mind

Places I have never seen and times of long ago

Seem to drive my hand to write as the north wind drives the snow

Castles out of fantasy and legends I have heard

Come alive within my mind and somehow become my words

Echoes dance and whisper and tell secrets of the past

Do they seek the written word to make the memories last

I know not what brings the words or what tales they may bring

Still I pause and listen and hear the echoes ring.

Table of Contents

Cheating

A month out on the highway and it's time that I went home

Lately I have noticed that my eyes have begun to roam

There was a waitress in Tulsa that sure filled out her top

She sent me some signals that she wanted me to stop

A lady in Calgary with tight jeans and a ponytail

Was sending me a signal that with her I could not fail

Yet still I travel onward in my truck so alone

Waiting for the special load that will take me home

A lady waits for me there to hold me thru the night

How I long to kiss her and hold her oh, so tight

Still I will travel onward and I wonder if she would mind

Could I cheat a little bit but only in my mind

Northern Nights

Stars light up the heavens, like candles in the night
Northern lights are flashing with a pale and ghostly light

Snow sparkles in the darkness, piled deep within the pines
An ice bound stream is silent, its waters dark as wine

Cold takes your breath away and chills you to the bone
The highway winds and wanders, so dark and all alone

My engine sings out deep and strong and pulls me ever on
My tires churn the drifting snow, ever northward sings their song

Why does this land so dark and cold fill me with such delight
Perhaps I feel the hand of God beneath these Northern Lights.

Passing Instant

The silence of the lonely night is broken by a sound

A big rig's diesel engine seems to shake the frozen ground

Headlights pierce the darkness with a clear unwavering light

They seem to cut a tunnel thru the dark and snowy night

Chrome glistens in the darkness lit by an amber glow

Red sparkles from the taillights thru the softly falling snow

A driver safe within his cab gently grips the wheel

Skillfully he guides his chariot of glass and chrome and steel

Tires whisper on the pavement and sing a sad and lonely song

Snow swirls with his passing; in an instant he is gone.

Serve and Protect

To serve and protect is how they make their pay

They place their lives upon the line each and every day

A car wreck takes a member's life; a bullet takes another

Left behind just memories for wives and dads and mothers

See the tears fall upon the flag, hear the single bugle play

The brotherhood of the badge lost another one today

A nation stands in silence and slowly bows their heads

Flags are lowered solemnly in honor of the dead

They serve and they protect, let them not die in vain

The brotherhood of the badge should never cry again

Whispering Wind

Out across the prairie the wind whispers to the grass

It speaks of what was said and done and what shall come to pass

Gentle breezes whisper about lazy summer nights

Of misty moonlight glow and the sparkle of starlight

Other breezes tell the tale of wind and snow and rain

Of the changing of the seasons and how it will come again

Tales of many travelers, what they have seen and what they
have done

In the darkness of the night or beneath a blazing sun

Tales of the good and bad, the future and the past

I listen to the whispering wind tell its secrets to the grass

The Last Load

Alone out in the trailer yard he crumpled to his knees

Tried so hard to get his breath and whispered, "Not here, please."

Pain blurred his vision as he opened up the door

One hand reached for the wheel and he gasped,
"Just three feet more."

He collapsed into the seat and fumbled for the key

Then he heard the engine roar and he whispered, "Now let it be."

We found him in the morning, hands clenched upon the wheel

Eyes fixed on the horizon and his skin as gray as steel

He went the way he wanted, with his boots upon his feet

His hands upon the steering wheel, sitting in the driver's seat

We buried him just today, with his logbook by his side

God, when you go to judge him, remember that he loved to drive.

Warning or Promise

I had a dream the other night that I was dead and gone
I had left this mortal world and I had traveled on

I stood before the final judge, prepared to have my say
For all the things that I had done I was prepared to pay

All the people I had hurt and the ones that I'd caused pain
Now stood to have their say and listed my sins again

My sins piled upon the scales for everyone to see
It wasn't looking very good for the sinner who was me

Then a single angel's feather floated down from up above
Followed by a teardrop from someone I had loved

The scales now reached a balance and the gates were opened wide
Saint Peter took me by the hand and welcomed me inside

That was when I awoke to face another dawn
On my pillow was a feather but when I reached out, it was gone

Could this have been a warning or was a promise made
I guess that I will never know until they lay me in my grave

For now I will try to do my best, live the best I can
I'll try to balance out the scales yet I am but a man

I know that I will make mistakes but still I have to try
Until I face that final judge in that courtroom in the sky.

You Touched Me

The very moment that we met, gently did we touch

Shyly we shook hands; it did not seem like much

You gently took me by the hand as I led you out to dance

My heart was beating faster and my brain said, "Take a chance."

That night you gave me our first kiss and I felt your lips on mine

As you gently touched me with your lips as sweet as wine

Much later on another night your touch set me on fire

We held each other thru the night filled with our desire

Then that evening in the church with you all gowned in white

You reached out your hand to mine and became my wife that night

So quickly now the years have passed and many things have
come to be

Yet I cannot forget you reached out and you touched me.

A Moment's Rest

High upon a mountain pass surrounded by ice and snow

A driver sits within his rig and checks the highway far below

His engine whispers softly and seems to warn him of the danger

Yet a schedule he must keep, no longer can he linger

A hand grips the steering wheel; gently it seems to say

Slow and steady wins the race, caution rules the day

Now tires whisper across the snow as the rig moves slowly on

A hint of diesel fills the air and in an instant they are gone.

Grandpa

Hands that were like steel backed by an iron will

Gone now for so many years yet I remember still

A quiet and a simple man who lived a simple life

Lived for his God, his country, his children and his wife

His word was a sacred bond and his handshake was a deal

Honest as the day was long, he would never cheat or steal

Had himself a little still by the creek down near the barn

Drank himself a little shine, but never caused any harm

He taught me how to spit, cast a fly and shoot a gun

To stand up for my beliefs and never shirk or run

Never did I kiss him or tell him of my love

Yet I know he's watching from somewhere up above

Would he be proud of who I am and how I have played the game?

Pop, I've always tried my best to hold up this family's name.

The Harbor

Alone upon the sea of life with his canvas torn and lost

A man struggles onward, no matter what the cost

Ahead a haven beckons; he sees the harbor light

A place of peace and blessing; a shelter from the night

Alone upon a different course with her canvas lost and torn

A woman struggles onward, adrift upon life's storm

Ahead a haven beckons; she sees the harbor light

A place of peace and blessing; a shelter from the night

Sheltered in the harbor two ships join together

Anchored by each other they will withstand any weather

Now they will sail together across the storms of life

Joined now in the sight of God as husband and as wife.

Lost Tears

Lightning strikes and thunder roars followed by the rain

Washing away my teardrops and leaving behind the pain

The many tears that I have shed, for daughters and for sons

Killed by senseless violence, by knife, car, drugs, or guns

Broken bodies in the street struck down by speeding cars

Drug addicts in the alley, behind some local bar

A woman and a little child cut down in a heap

Victims of a turf war, a drive-by in the street

A bomb explodes and many die in some far and distant land

Their blood and their dreams soaked up by the sand

A child somehow gets a gun and goes on a killing spree

A husband kills his wife and child because he wants to be free

My tears for all the innocent are washed out by the rain

The thunder and the lightning underscore the pain.

Friends

The highways wind and wander; the seasons come and go
The four lanes and the two lanes, the sun, the rain and the snow

The years just seem to slip away and this highway has no end
Always there is another hill or there is another bend

The many places I have seen all seem to run together
The many seasons I have seen, just categorized as weather

Yet I have met so many people and so very many friends
They are the reason that I travel this road that never ends

Friends are like a beacon that helps to guide you on your way
Their smiles are like a summer breeze upon a winter's day

As long as I still have friends I'll stay out on this street
There are so very many friends that I have yet to meet

Old Drivers

Old Russ finally hung up the keys, and Fred, he quit last year

Don and Art and Andy, well, their retirement dates are near

The drivers are all changing and the road is not the same

We are the last of a dying breed yet we still play the game

The old trucks are all gone; their steel has turned to rust

Many drivers followed them and their bodies are now dust

Some of us still struggle on and try to keep the dream alive

We try to teach the new breed how to act and how to drive

Old Knights of the highway with our armor bent and rusted

Stagger off to our steeds though our bodies are tired and busted

Once more into the breach; haul just one more load

Ride into the sunset on that never-ending road.

Tears

I pull out of the driveway and I see her wave goodbye

I can see the tears upon her face though I asked her not to cry

I give the horn a little toot as I grab another gear

Now my eyes are misty and on my cheek there is a tear

I see her in the mirror getting smaller all the time

I give thanks for what I have and for this life of mine

Yes on my cheek there is a teardrop but within me is a smile

I will keep her memory with me across every lonely mile

Now I turn that first corner and her figure disappears

Why is this road so misty and can I blame it on her tears?

War

Oh listen to that bugle call and hear the drummers play

An army marches off to war with cheering crowds along the way

Oh listen to the rifles fire and hear the mighty cannon roar

Battle is joined, armies advance, and men fall by the score

Oh listen to the single drum and hear that lonely bugler play

Widows cry among the stones, the men came home today

Home Tonight

The house is finally quiet and the children are asleep in bed

Her old dog slowly wags his tail as she gently strokes his head

She thinks back over her day and makes plans for her tomorrow

Wonders what it may bring, happiness or sorrow

She waits for the phone to ring from her trucker on the road

Will he be coming home or will he pull another load

The dog's ears perk up suddenly as he heads for the door

Now his tail wags joyously as he bounds across the floor

Now she also hears a noise, a sharp and rapping sound

The sound made by a Jake brake as a big old truck gears down

Headlights flash across the house and pull up in the drive

Her heart is beating faster and her house has come alive

Children tumble from their beds shouting, "Daddy's home!"

The old dog backs excitedly like he'd just found a bone

Now she is in his arms again and all her world is right

Stars twinkle in the heavens, the trucker's home tonight.

Letter to a Trucker's Wife

It's time we had a little talk about the one you call your man

I know how much you love him but I'll steal him if I can

You know even when he's with you thoughts of me are in his head

But then I've heard him call your name when he is in my bed

He calls me his baby and he holds me oh, so tight

He whispers secrets to me as we travel thru the night

He buys me lots of little things and he loves to see me shine

I take him places that you can't in my bid to make him mine

Don't try to use your children, you see they like me too

But even when they are with me I know they are missing you

I realize you love him and I wish you lots of luck

Just remember he is also mine, sincerely, signed The Truck.

Gentle Breezes

Gentle winds caress us beneath the shade tree where we lie

Clouds like fluffy pillows drift across a gentle sky

A brook murmurs softly as it wanders on its way

In the branches high above us a little squirrel plays

A lady lies beside me and places her hand in mine

We drift off in peaceful dreams in this gentle summertime

Dreams of love and laughter beneath a summer sun

Dreams about a gentle love as hand in hand we run

Dreams of summers in the past before our hair turned gray

Yet we return again to this blanket where we lay

Our lives and love runs slower now but still runs true and deep

Gentle breezes kiss us in the meadow where we sleep

Trilogy

Daddy

Take me by the hand and walk thru this world with me
Teach me how to live and love and show me what you see

Teach me what I need to know and hold me in your arms
Help me with your wisdom and keep me safe from harm

Father
Take me by the hand and walk thru this world with me
Teach me what I need to know and help me with what I see

Protect me as I raise my child in this world of pain and strife
Help me with your wisdom as I struggle thru this life

Children
Reach out and take my hand and walk thru this world with me
I will be there to guide you, just open your hearts to me

Those that chose to follow me; their lives are not in vain
They will live forever in a world that knows no pain

My Journey

I have roamed and wandered and many places I have seen

I've slept in a hobo jungle and I've stood before a Queen

I have paddled a canoe across lakes and rivers wide

I've rode a sturdy buckskin with a rifle by my side

Soared above the clouds, held aloft on man-made wings

Heard the lonesome whistle blow and I've heard the tires sing

I've ridden in a horse-drawn sleigh and watched as man walked
on the moon

Wandered the Arctic's ice and snow and seen the desert
in full bloom

Crossed the Atlantic and Pacific in ships made out of steel

Seen about five million miles across a steering wheel

Yes I have loved and lost and I have fought and won

Still my only claim to fame is my daughter and my son

Victories have come and gone and friends have done the same

The only legacy I leave will be my family's name

A footnote in the sands of time, just one single little grain

Yet if I could do it all again I'd do everything the same.

Morning at the Lake

Not a ripple mars the surface in the stillness of the dawn

The stars' twinkle ghostly; shimmer, then are gone

The reflection in the water mirrors the hills and trees

The world seems to slow waiting for a morning breeze

In the distance hear the lonesome loon call his plaintive cry

Hear it echo off the hills and bounce across the sky

The morning stillness of the lake echoes thru my mind

I sit and drink my coffee and let my soul unwind

Ghost Drivers

An old truck driver headed out one dark and windy day
He rested on a lonely ridge as he went on his way

All at once a convoy of big old trucks he saw
Coming across the ragged sky and up a cloudy draw

Their stacks were belching fire and their bumpers were of steel
As the first truck rushed on by him its hot breath he could feel

He could see the drivers coming hard on that road up in the sky
He could see them fight their steering wheels and he heard their
mournful cry

Yippee I ahhhhh Yippee I oooh
Ghost drivers in the sky

As the drivers rushed on by him he heard one call his name
If you want to save your soul from Hell and driving on this range

Then driver change your way of life or with us you will drive
Trying to haul the Devil's freight across these endless skies

Their faces burned, their eyes are red, their shirts all
soaked in sweat
Try hard to make a deadline but they ain't made it yet

Doomed to drive forever across those endless skies
Their diesels snorting fire as they drive on hear their cry

Yippee I aahhhh Yippee I ooohhh
Ghost drivers in the sky

23

My Lady Sleeps

She lies there quietly sleeping as I watch her in the dark

Deep inside I wonder does she know what's in my heart

Can she even realize how much I really care

Is there some way to tell her as I watch her lying there

Does she know she is my sunshine and the stars that light my sky

I know not how to tell her though many times I've tried

I, like so many other men, cannot say what's in my heart

Many times I've tried to tell her but I know not how to start

I'll just lie here quietly and hold her thru the night

Slip away in peaceful dreams until the morning light

Simple Faith

A simple little country church on a gentle summer morn
Its choir sings the old songs and a life-long faith is born

Amazing Grace and The Rugged Cross,
Rock of Ages Cleft for Me,
Stories from the ages of a man that calmed the sea

Songs sung just a bit off-key but coming from the heart
Young and old together, each one sings a part

Seated in hand-made pews with church windows of plain glass
A pulpit made of local pine and a cross of hammered brass

Just another simple country church surrounded by the pines
A simple place for simple folk,
Faith that will stand the test of time.

Twister

Dark clouds blot out the sun and thunder rocks the sky

A funnel reaches for the ground, rotates from up on high

Lightning flashes, thunder rolls and wind now drives the rain

Hailstones bounce across the land and thunder rolls again

Darkness reaches for the ground, roars like a speeding train

Branches and trees are ripped apart and thunder rolls again

The funnel now begins to dance, to shift and jump and sway

It spreads destruction in its path like a devil child at play

Homes and buildings ripped apart, trees torn from the ground

A loaded semi tossed aside, debris thrown all around

It path is pure destruction and lives are torn asunder

Then in an instant it is gone and again we hear the thunder

.

A Trucker's Weekend

New trucks, old trucks, trucks from big to small

Gatherings of the very best as the truckers have a ball

A weekend meeting old friends and making new ones too

Stories of the trip from Hell and tales of derring-do

The smell of burning rubber as diesel smoke rolls black

The thunder of the engines from the big rigs on the track

Show trucks shining brightly, work trucks scrubbed and clean

Old trucks and the new trucks, like something from a dream

A young child shines a bumper; a poodle sniffs a wheel

Companies hand out brochures and try to swing a deal

Music in the darkness as truckers dance and sing

A weekend to celebrate where the driver is a king

A respite from the highway as pro truckers take a rest

A time to get together and be with the very best.

Black Water

Black water Mountain Lake, your waters still and deep

Down in your shadowed depths, what secrets do you keep?

Deep within your morning mists do shadows dance and sway?

Souls of the lives you have claimed held here until judgment day.

That quiet Indian hunter, on thin ice he tried to cross,

Was there wailing in his lodge when his life was lost?

Perhaps there was a lover who had cheated just one time?

They never found the body as they only searched the pines.

Your deep mysterious waters whisper to my mind,

Yet they will keep their secrets until the end of time.

Gentle Rain

Rain falls upon my sleeper and I feel gentle breezes blow,

Gray invades my solitude and my truck rocks oh so slow.

Encased in my cocoon of steel, not asleep, yet not awake.

I lie and listen to the rain yet I have miles to make.

Still I need my quiet times when I may rest and think,

Other things sustain a man, not just food and drink.

My empty arms long to be home and I call her name again,

A single tear rolls down my cheek as I listen to the rain.

Another Hill

My diesel engine thunders as we climb the great divide,

I wonder what awaits me there on the other side?

Perhaps there will be clouds and rain as I travel down the road,

Perhaps there will be slick spots and I may dump my load.

Each trip along the highway seems to reflect my life,

Today there may be sunshine and tomorrow may bring strife.

The miles roll out behind me, ever onward come what may.

Clouds will come and clouds will go as I travel on my way.

I have my share of sunshine, time to laugh and play

Each journey like my life I must face day by day.

My engine slows its thunder as we start down the other side,

I settle deeper in the seat and pray for a long, long ride.

Hard Facts

Why is it that some are so blind that they cannot see?
The forest right in front of them because they are looking
for a tree?

You try to help some people and give them good advice,
Yet when it is time to act they will not pay the price.

Relationships mean compromise especially in a trucker's life
Sometimes the load comes first, before the family or the wife.

We do our best to make it home but at times we must pass that gate
The company does not ever care unless the load is late.

Industry does not care about our families at any time,
Birthdays and holidays will not help their bottom line.

Don't expect a trucker home until he parks it in the drive,
Then do your best while he is home to keep the love alive.

Communication is the key when he is on the road,
Do your best to make it light; cares make for a heavy load.

Freight is always moving and it makes for a hard old life,
The ones that it is hardest on are the children and the wife.

They are the ones who sit at home, they worry and they wait.
That trucker he will soon be home, truckers are never late.

Birth Of A Wild One

On legs that tremble wildly he stumbles to his feet,

In only minutes he must run, survival lies in speed.

His mother stands that he may feed, then slowly leads him
on his way.

If he is to live they must move, there is no time to play.

His legs are getting stronger now and in moments he can run,

Other colts now run beside him and they gallop in the sun.

High above them on a ridge his sire sniffs the air,

Ever on guard for dangers that may strike him or his heir.

The herd now moves together as I sit here in the sun,

I witnessed a wild one's birth and I watch the wild ones run.

Silent Flight

I soar aloft on sunlit wings and my tow rope falls away.

I turn and bank towards the ridge, in the thermals I will play.

Lifted high by God's elevator I soar across the sky,

Silent in my solitude, like an Eagle do I fly.

I turn and bank among the clouds and chase sunbeams
across the sky,

I dive now like a stooping Hawk then climb back up on high.

Time and gravity intrude and I must return to land,

I put aside my sunlit wings and place my feet back in the sand.

I have soared with Eagles and chased my dreams across the sky,

In my mind I will return to the silence of the sky.

Painted Sky

No master painter with a brush could match a sunset sky,

Or the glory of a sunrise that lights a cloudy sky.

What man could watch a sunset over the Great Divide,

Then look me in the face and say God is not alive?

Perhaps in these times of stress when men must fight and die,

Could the answer lie before us across a painted sky?

If foes could but stand together and see the wonders
God has made,

Would they be so eager to face an early grave?

I stand and face the rising sun and watch a painted sky,

God paints another masterpiece as the clouds drift slowly by.

The Show Truck

Paint, all washed and waxed and shiny, chrome buffed
until it gleams,

Rubber shining dark and black like something from a dream.

Lights shining bright as crystal, a windshield without a bug,

A rose upon the pillow, no oil stains on the rug.

Show trucks in all their splendor shining in the sun,

Yet Monday they will roll again on another endless run.

Windshields will be splattered with bugs, paint streaked
with dirt and oil,

Just today they take a rest from their never-ending toil.

The Smokin' Gun

Anticipation in the pits, Crowds have gathered around,

A diesel engine comes to life and shakes the very ground.

Slowly to the starting line, the crowd begins to cheer.

Smoke and noise and speed brings them from far and near.

Smoke billows from the tires, the stacks blow clouds of black.

The crowd comes to their feet as he eases slowly back.

He edges to the starting line, his eyes upon the tree,

Then as the green light flashes he sets the monster free.

Two thousand horses come to life, the smoke obscures the sun.

The Smokin' Gun tears down the track on his twelve second run.

Pacific Waters

North Pacific waters, cold, dark and deep,

Cliffs rise from the shore, hard, tall and steep.

Valleys shrouded deep in mist, home of the Spirit Bear,

Rivers filed with Salmon where Eagles rule the air.

Forests dark with growing pine nurtured by the rain,

Rocky gravel beaches where the waves crash home again.

Totems of the old ones lie fallen in the pines,

Villages lie flattened, ravaged by wind and time.

Yet still the darkened waters slowly slip on by,

Wind curls around the peaks, clouds sail across the sky.

A land steeped in mystery, ocean, sky and pine,

A picture from a bygone age, a moment out of time.

Bonds

We walk across the sands of time as many have before,

The future stretches out ahead like the opening of a door.

From here we all will scatter each to go our separate way.

Let us all remember those we meet along the way.

Teachers, friends and classmates will soon be left behind,

Soon to be just shadows in the recess of our minds.

Some will go on to college while others heed the bugle's call.

Some will stay behind yet we must remember all.

Bonds we have formed together are something that will last.

As we travel onward we must not forget the past.

Wintry Haven

The cold cuts to the bone, stars burn clear and bright.

Northern Lights are flashing in the darkness of the night.

A cabin nestles in the pines, windows all aglow,

Lamplight paints a golden path across the sparkling snow.

Smoke spirals from the chimney, inside a fire burns bright.

A haven in the darkness of a cold and wintry night.

A cabin in the north woods, a place of warmth and light,

A simple place of shelter on a cold December night.

The Poet

Always searching for himself, alone in a crowded land,

Marching to his own beat, he hears a different band.

He dreams of Knights and Dragons and rescues the Lady Fair,

Then takes her off to live with him in a castle in the air.

He has stories of a cowboy, a horse, a gun and saddle,

Life on the western plains rounding up the cattle.

His spaceship flies among the stars to worlds no man has seen,

Atmospheres no man can breathe with seas of pink and green.

He can take us with him with his paper and his pen,

We wander through his many worlds then we come home again.

Yet he keeps on searching as he wanders across the land,

Marching to a different drum, he hears a different band.

Gently Falling Rain

I watch a child splash through a puddle, feel the mud ooze
'neath his feet,

I hear the cars go driving by and hear the tires hiss on the street.

A mother bird settles on her nest to protect her fragile eggs.

Flowers seem to raise their heads, their stems like little legs.

A dog goes running by and stops to give a shake,

A duck now goes waddling by to lead her ducklings to the lake.

The whole world seems washed and clean and the air
smells fresh again,

I sit in quiet solitude in the gently falling rain.

Northerner

This north wind blows so very cold
        My pony stumbles then moves on

The snow is drifting deeper
        Will we live to see the dawn?

Cattle are scattered by the wind
        I'll save the ones I can.

My pony stumbles once again
        The reins freeze to my hand.

My feet feel like a block of ice
        I give my horse his head.

I pray that he will find his way,
        Or we may wind up dead.

My pony struggles onward,
        Do I see a hint of light?

The barn is there in front of us,
        God, this wind is cold tonight!

Blue Lagoon

I wander thru the wilderness, land of eagle, wolf and bear.

The forest and the seacoast. What secrets lie hidden there?

This land, so harsh, yet beautiful, what secrets does it keep?

Its forests so dark and green, its waters so dark and deep.

Eagles soar high overhead, wolves raise their mournful cry.

Bears roam across the land, salmon spawn, then die.

Nature has a rhythm set by the sun and moon,

I sit and watch the seasons beside this blue lagoon.

Camp Out

Stars sparkle in the heavens, clear and hard and bright,

A full moon rides a darkened sky, gives a misty, ghostly light.

A shadow glides across the meadow on swift and silent wings,

A Great Horned Owl is hunting for mice and other things.

Far off in the distance I can hear a wild Wolf howl.

Darkness falls across the land, night's hunters are on the prowl.

My campfire crackles softly and gives a soothing light,

My mind begins to wander in the stillness of the night.

Quiet breezes whisper through the tall and stately pines,

Mother Nature's gentle magic soothes my fevered mind.

Sound

Why did all the little birds somehow cease their song

They were a constant pleasure that I heard all day long.

Dogs' voices are now muted and telephones don't ring

I cannot hear the voices of children when they sing.

Still I see the wonders but I do not hear the sound,

Silence, once a fleeting thing, now comes from all around.

Years with a roaring diesel and the rumble of the road

Somehow stole a part of me and left me in the cold.

No more do I hear the whisper of a lover in the night

Still I can see her face, I have not lost my sight.

I will struggle onward and be all that I can be,

Still I miss the little birds singing wild and free.

Dark Journey

I danced with the Devil, a needle in my veins

Saw the sun set in the east through smoky cloudy dreams.

Lost days and weeks to alcohol and tripped across the sky.

The Devil sat beside me as we watched a good friend die.

I've woken up in the gutter of an alley cold and dark,

Mugged a drunken homeless man for two bucks in the park.

I've seen the very worst of life and at times have prayed for death,

Yet I always struggled onward and took another faltering breath.

Now someone has come to me, reached out and taken my hand,

He raised me from the gutter and taught me how to stand.

My sins have been forgiven and I will never walk alone,

With help from God and others I've found my way back home.

The Cruise

We sailed away on a ship of fools, a one-eyed cat and I,

Sailed east toward the setting sun as fish flew through the sky.

The Captain was a drunken fool and the first mate he was worse,

The cook jumped ship as we sailed away and I knew this trip
was cursed.

The cat and I stole a lifeboat and flew off toward the moon,

The cat he dined on flying fish while I sang a happy tune.

We flew off to a desert land and crashed in a big Oak tree.

The cat went mad and swam away and now all is left is me.

I sit and dine on the chocolate trees and drink from the cola spring.

Play baseball with the flying fish and wonder what will
tomorrow bring.

The Whispering Sands

I sit quietly and listen to the shifting whispering sand,

It tells me tales of all that passed as it traveled across the land.

Tales of a Viking long ship and the men that plied its oars.

How they rested long ago here on these foreign shores

Tales of fishermen in barques and little tiny ships,

How they rested and replenished here on their perilous trips.

Tales of the natives that came to these shifting shores,

Of all the catches that they made for their winter stores.

Tales of ships that were torn apart by storms that wracked the sea,

Their bones lie hidden in the sand where no one will ever see.

Tales of those that come to see the beauty of this land

Those that will sit and listen to the shifting whispering sand

Cold Winds

A wind cold as a dagger chills me to the bone,

Huddled down behind a rock, my thoughts return to home.

I dream of those I left behind, my family and my friends

I pray I will return to them when this horror ends.

Then I clear my mind to the task that lies ahead,

I have no time for thoughts of home; this rock must be my bed.

Darkness all around me, shadows shift and sway,

My family now is those I guard and it is for them I pray.

We battle in this foreign land, a land so stark and fierce,

We fight only because we must so the world may be at peace.

I am but a common soldier who has his dreams of home,

This wind cuts like a dagger and chills me to the bone.

Darling

Darling ----- my sweet darling, take me in your arms,
won't you please

Darling --- precious darling, kiss me one more time before I leave.

This life we lived together has been filled with joy and pain,

If it was in my power, I would do it all again.

Through all the ups and downs of life you were right there
by my side,

How fitting you should be with me as I take my final ride.

Standing there beside you is an Angel dressed in white

Do not shed your tears for me on this our final night.

Darling ----- my sweet darling, take me in your arms now,
won't you please

Darling --- precious darling, kiss me now, it's time for me to leave.

The Entertainer

He steps out on a dingy stage, sings songs from the past.

He has his dreams and memories, the only thing that lasts.

He is singing all the old songs that were hits so long ago,

Yet some still sit and listen until it's time for him to go.

He staggers down off the stage to an old van parked out back,

Tomorrow is another show, somewhere down the track.

Just another entertainer with another nameless band,

They travel ever onward across a cold uncaring land.

Worship

Forget the stained glass windows, the towers to the sky,

Forget the massive organs and bells pealing up on high.

I have no need for towers or icons made of gold,

Floors of teak or marble are all so dead and cold.

Give me instead a mountain lake, a meadow or a tree,

I need no walls around me to set my spirits free.

I'll worship underneath the sky, not beneath electric lights,

Stars will be my ceiling, like candles in the night.

A fallen log will be my pew, the wind will be my choir,

I can hear the voice of God in the crackle of my fire.

Another Trip

Pavement stretches out ahead of him as he pulls out of the gate,

The load he has just picked up is already one day late.

The shipper, he blames dispatch, dispatch just doesn't care,

They all will blame the driver whenever he gets there.

The driver grabs another gear as his rig comes up to speed,

Coffee, time and diesel fuel are the only things he needs.

Linked now by the asphalt to others of his kind,

The driver sits and ponders the questions in his mind.

Thoughts of his friends and family and those that he holds dear.

Pushed firmly to the side as he grabs another gear.

The rhythm of the high road now has him in its grip,

Another lonely driver on another lonely trip.

She Trembles

She trembles in the darkness, frightened and alone,
Wanders through the cluttered rooms of what was a loving home.

What happened to her dreams and plans,
what tore her world apart?

Where did he find the hateful words that struck to her very heart?

A love that burnt like raging fire, now ashes of despair,
Only honor warms her now and fear is what holds her there.

She cannot break the vows she gave,
a promise made to keep,

Yet now she must weigh the cost and the price may be too steep.

The price could be her sanity or perhaps her very life,
She trembles in the darkness in the midst of all this strife.

In the darkness comes a ray of light
as a friend reaches out a hand,

Steadies her and dusts her off and helps her now to stand.

Before her now are pathways that she must walk alone.
One leads off around a bend and the other takes her home.

The choice ahead is hers alone,
the road is hers to tread.

Will she kneel and tremble or will she move ahead?

Friends are there to help her, aid her if she may fall,
Yet now the choice is hers alone, no one else can make this call.

The God of Battle

He has traveled through the ages, walked across the sands of time.

His footprints you see today are covered by a sandy slime.

He's been in sodden jungles and walked the barren sand,

Friend and foe he's left behind touched by his bloody hand.

From the dawn of history up to the present day,

The bodies of the fallen lie strewn along the way.

Both famous men and nameless men struggled, and then fell.

No one can know the things he's seen here in his living hell.

Gods have lived and Gods have died, nations have risen; fell,

How very many men have died, no one can ever tell.

Is he a force of evil? Does he know right from wrong?

This bloody God of Battle has ruled for much too long.

Yet still he struggles onward his body dripping red,

He is the God of Battle and he stands among the dead.

Furry Friends

They sit there in the shotgun seat like kings upon a throne,

We work to secure our loads while they gnaw on a bone.

Then as we travel down the road they need to check a tire,

They do a dance between the seats like something may be on fire.

We pull over to the side and they check every weed,

Sometimes it takes a half an hour to do a one minute deed.

They need their food and water then if you stop to eat,

You don't dare forget them so you bring them back a treat.

They care not if you profit or if you take a loss.

They sit there in the shotgun seat – I wonder who's the boss???

Beyond the Sunset

The time has almost come that we will be forced to part,

Though I will travel on ahead, I know I'll stay within your heart.

I'll go ahead to blaze a trail but I'll not travel far,

Just beyond the sunset I'll camp by the evening star.

If you ever feel too lonely just look up into the night,

The evening star will be my campfire and I know you'll see
the light,

There will be no need to grieve for I'll not be far away,

Just beyond the sunset, the star will light the way.

When it is your time to go just reach out and take my hand,

Together we will cross over into the promised land.

Let Me Escape

Take me back to another time before the whole world changed,

When we all lived in villages and knew each others' names.

Life was so much slower then and Mother Nature set the pace,

Horsepower came with hooves and there was no need to race.

Let me walk down dusty roads and smell the new-mown hay,

Let me sail a little fishing boat across a misty bay.

Let me tarry in the stable with a quiet gentle Clyde,

Wander thru a woodland with an old dog by my side.

Let me sit upon a mountain and feel gentle breezes blow,

Walk arm in arm with my true love thru gently falling snow.

Let me escape into a dream of a whole world fresh and new,

Peaceful days and quiet nights and gently falling dew.

Dreamland

Join me in a dream of a magical mystical land,

Walk with me along the shore, barefoot in the sand.

Stroll with me thru a forest green to a quiet peaceful stream.

Bathe with me in waters pure then dry in warm sunbeams.

Let's stroll across the meadow to a cottage 'neath a pine.

Sit with me at the table and sip some apple wine.

Lay with me upon a bed as soft as thistle down,

Spread your hair on the pillow, weave moonbeams for your gown.

Let our minds slip off in dreams and wake to a brand new day,

Chase butterflies in the meadow and join children as they play.

Come with me into a dream of magic and mystery,

A dream I made for us to share, just for you and me.

Harvest

Mornings with a touch of frost, days still warm and bright.

The trees are changing color and a fog rolls in at night.

Farmers reap their harvest of golden corn and grain

The echo of the wild goose rings thru the sky again.

Wild flowers in the meadow drop their seed upon the ground,

Grasses in the meadow dry and turn to brown.

Fruit ripens in the orchard; there is the scent of new-mown hay.

A deer slips thru the forest to watch the squirrels as they play.

Bees drone among the flowers and hurry to their hive,

Collecting for the days ahead to keep their young alive.

The world reaps the bounty of Mother Nature's hand,

Then slows to another tempo before winter takes the land.

The Gentle Wind

The wind whispers to me as it travels across the land.

It sings as it whispers and gently moves the sand.

The sand moves and covers dreams of another time.

Yet still the gentle wind whispers to my mind.

Tales of time and ages past and stories yet untold,

Tales of suffering and pain and tales of jewels and gold.

Of men and how they struggled, their comrades by their side,

The children and the pioneers and how they lived and died.

One just must sit and listen to the gentle knowing wind.

It whispers, how it whispers, just like a long-lost friend.

It tells me all the secrets of times so long ago,

I sit and listen to the wind, gently does it blow.

Circles

People in their multitudes, short, tall, fat and lean,

Rushing, ever rushing from scene to shifting scene.

I sit and watch as they rush by, always on the go,

Are they moving for a reason or do they even know.

Like a flock of little birds, they wheel and twist and turn,

I sit and watch them endlessly as their energy they burn.

Left, then right, then back again, an endless ebbing flow,

Circles within circles as up and down they go.

From home to work then back again, schedule time to play,

Then time to sleep and time to eat within their busy day.

A never-ending whirl of time, but I have stepped aside.

I sit and watch the others as on and on they ride.

A Dreamer

In the midst of a bustling crowd is a quiet lonely man,

Overwhelmed by the crowds he does the best he can.

Mostly unnoticed by the crowd he struggles to survive,

Somehow he must protect himself and keep his dreams alive.

Dreams of peace and harmony where no one walks in fear

Can his vision ever work with the things that he sees here?

Yet, around him ripples spread like water on a lake,

Maybe his dream will come to pass but oh, the time it takes.

A dreamer, he stands alone, just another man.

Yet dreams are part of this world, part of nature's plan.

The Pickup

Hidden back behind the barn, covered by the weeds,

An old pickup turns to rust, forgotten are her deeds.

That night back in Fifty-two, head lights burning bright,

She took a lady to the hospital and a child was born that night.

That time in Fifty-four when floods covered the land,

She splashed thru the water hauling bags of sand.

Hay bales, oats, grain and corn she hauled in from the field.

Along with the fruits and vegetables that the land did yield.

Three children she taught to drive; oh her tortured gears,

Many were her scrapes and dents she suffered thru the years.

Her motor went in Fifty-nine, the tranny in Sixty-two,

A body job in Sixty- three made her feel like new.

Time and tide wait for no one and metal turns to rust,

Now she sits out behind the barn covered up with dust.

Now a young man has come with another plan,

Soon she will be a show piece and in glory she will stand.

A new life of ease with love and care,

If only she could talk, what memories she could share.

The Terrorist

Hidden among society like a cancer of the soul,

A terrorist plots his deadly deeds, his eyes upon his goal.

Freedom is not in his game, he lives for hate and fear,

Destruction is his way of life and death always hovers near.

Yet he is a coward who does not wish to fight,

Like a rat he cowers in the cover of the night.

Explosives are his tool of choice and the innocent his prey.

His dreams are dreams of power where the innocent must pay.

If we win we live in freedom, If he wins we live as slaves.

If we win the stars are our home, if he wins, we live in caves.

Now is the time to make a choice, Which one will it be?

Me – I made my choice, if I die I'll at least die free.

Feeding

I have seen the Arctic snow and sailed the seven seas,

Crossed the arid desert and stood beneath jungle trees.

I've sailed along beside a Whale and heard a Lion roar.

Seen the strangest animals and birds, by sea, and on the shore.

I dove among the fishes and watched a White Shark feed,

Held Hummingbirds in my hand and fed a Chipmunk seed.

I've stood among the mighty and I've sat among the meek,

Watched as they did their feeding with tooth and claw and beak.

Many things I've seen and done yet I remember best,

Sitting with a mother with a baby at her breast.

A scene so soft and wonderful, of peace and boundless love,

Sent down from our maker who is watching from above.

The Other Woman

Yes there is another woman I've been spending some time with,

A special little lady that has a lot to give.

Don't look at her as a rival, rather see her as a friend.

You know that you're the one I'll be with until the end.

But, she carries me to places that you have never been,

She has been with me through problems that you have never seen.

I tell her all about you as I cross the lonely miles,

All the time I spend with her, I'd trade for just your smile.

Still she has her moments and I'm often in her bed.

Even there the thoughts of you are running through my head.

Now please don't cry my darling, I think you may be in luck,

The fact of the matter is, the other woman is a truck.

Ageing

When I got up this morning I noticed something strange,

The youthful face I used to shave has undergone a change.

What put those lines upon my face and the gray that's in my hair?

There's gray in my mustache now, how did that get there?

I find that I'm still growing but in a different way,

Surely my jeans are shrinking, they get smaller every day.

The type is getting smaller in everything I read.

It must be a conspiracy, now who would do that deed?

I guess I must put up with it, these ravages of time,

Live with all these aches and pains, and learn to make them mine.

The Waitress

Stopped at a little truckstop just the other day.

Another line drawn in my log as I travel along my way.

The waitress was real busy, but she poured my coffee with a grin,

Told me a joke, shared a laugh, made me glad that I'd dropped in.

This lady I will remember as I pass along my way,

A laugh, a grin, a little joke sure helps to make my day.

A waitress has a thankless job, long hours with little pay,

But they are the ones that bring us back as we travel on our way.

Our Ladies

They sit alone at home and wait sometimes with their tears,

We drive along the highways, our minds on shifting gears.

We hope that they will wait for us and this lifestyle that we live,

Then we return to them for the love they have to give.

The many things our ladies do, no man can understand.

They sit alone and wait for their truck-driving man.

They are the reason that we work, the reason that we drive,

They're the basis of our nation and they keep our world alive.

Wanderer

I have seen the Eagles soar, listened to Coyotes cry,

Heard the whisper of the pines, seen Ducks wheel across the sky.

I sat and watched a stately Elk and heard a Cougar scream.

I've watched a giant Grizzly fish in a Salmon stream.

Birds I've seen upon their nests, I've watched a Whitetail
giving birth.

Watched as lowly Ground Squirrels dug their home in
mother earth.

I've traveled and I've wandered oh, so far from home,

Yet with nature all around me I will never be alone.

The Logbook

His logbook's on the table, his keys are in the drawer,

His truck is parked on the lot, he won't need these things no more.

He left us just the other day on a trip we all must make,

To stand before the final court, their judgment he must take.

He will not stand and bow his head, he will hold his head up high,

He will face the final judge and he'll look him in the eye.

He will not make excuses, he's not that type of man,

Through his trials and tribulations, he always made a stand.

Yes he made a few mistakes, and for those he will pay the price.

One thing always sustained him, his faith in Jesus Christ.

Someday I hope to join him in that kingdom up on high

Remember when you judge him, how much he loved to drive.

His logbook is on the table, his keys are in the drawer.

The driver has gone home, he won't need them any more.

Three Trucks

Three trucks headed out tonight, each one has a tale.
As they rumble through the night they talk along the trail.

The first is a younger man, just starting on this run,
Six months he's been married, life to him is still fun.

Now he starts to worry, there's a baby on the way,
He's starting to realize the price he has to pay.

Out here on this highway with a wife at home,
It's hard to stay in touch with just a telephone.

The second he is older and divorced nigh on ten years,
He saw his marriage torn apart while he was shifting gears.

He worries about his children, He doesn't see them much at all,
He tries to give some guidance when he has time to call.

The third is not much different, I know because it's me,
Thirty years behind the wheel, still learning don't you see.

Thirty years of marriage yet I still love my bride,
She always travels with me, tucked down deep inside.

Three very different drivers each with his own load,
Can they learn from each other as they travel down the road.

Act of Kindness

He walked into the café, he felt so tired, old and gray
Thirty years of asphalt under his wheel today.

Marie, she saw him coming and she grabbed the coffee pot

Said, "Jake, I got what you need, strong and black and hot."

He slowly looked her up and down and said,
"Marie, you're quite a girl,
But what I need just isn't here, you won't find it in this world.

My wife left eight years ago, now she's with another man,

My children have all grown and left
so I get by the best I can."

Marie poured him a coffee and watched him where he sat,
Thought it was a crying shame to see old Jake like that.

Then when Jake got up to leave in front of twenty men,

Marie gave him a big old hug, said, "You best come back again."

Jake headed across the parking lot with
the spring back in his step,
As he climbed in his truck said, "Well, I ain't dead yet."

Now Jake's back on the highway smiling as he goes
down the road,

Just a simple act of kindness helped him bear his load.

The Mountain

There's a place up high on a mountain that I go when
no one's around,

A stream flows there on the mountain and I lose my cares
at its sound.

A breeze blows there on the mountain, I hear it sigh
through the pines,

A quiet voice softly whispers visions of peace
to my mind.

The brook running softly is laughter, the sun on my face
is a touch,

Nature in all of its wonder has given this mountain
so much.

Alone I come to this mountain with its rocks and pine trees
so high.

Nature gathers around me as I watch the
eagles fly.

Alone above the works of man I watch as the world
passes by,

I stand tall on the mountain, I reach and
touch the sky.

Cry Softly

I come home to you in the daytime, in the harsh daylight.

I touch you in the evening in the soft twilight.

I hold you in the darkness as the moon begins to rise.

I kiss you in the moon glow with the starlight in our eyes.

We love throughout the darkness in a long and endless night.

You kiss me in the morning mist and say that it's all right.

You hold me as the dawn breaks and whisper soft and low.

You touch me as I am leaving and cry softly as I go.

Birds

Have you listened to a Robin as he told the world of spring?

These are the same feelings that thoughts of you will bring.

Ever seen a Sparrow safe within her nest?

That's the way I feel when you hold me to your breast.

Have you ever heard a Loon call when his mate has gone astray?

That's the way that I feel when you have gone away.

Ever watched a Golden Eagle, seen how proudly he scans the land?

That's the way I feel when you take me by the hand.

What Mother Nature tells you if you stop and watch the birds

Are all the things I'd like to say if I only knew the words.

Valley of the Pines

I came down off a mountain to a valley lush and green,
The most peaceful valley that I had ever seen.

I stood beside a little lake, its water deep and still,
Watched as a snow white buffalo stopped and drank his fill

I watched a mighty cougar lie down beside a deer,
The peace of this green valley had touched the creatures here.

I watched as a lovely maiden bathed in a gentle stream.
This was the most idyllic spot my eyes had ever seen.

A reflection in the water. In buckskin I did stand,
Moccasins upon my feet and a feather in my hand.

Then I heard a gentle voice that welcomed me to stay,
Welcomed a weary traveler to rest for a night and day.

No longer could I linger as this was not my time,
But they said they had reserved my place in the Valley of the Pine.

Rested now the next day I go along my way,
Assured of my resting place where I could come another day.

I'll climb many mountains and return in my time,
Assured that I may rest in peace in the Valley of the Pine.

Last Stand

Alone upon a mesa beneath a cloudless sky,

A proud and noble warrior watches wagons rolling by.

He sees the end of all he knows here on this rugged plain,

The wagons forging westward, then next will come the train.

In his mind he sees the fences where once he used to roam,

The sad end of the buffalo and the strangling of his home.

Visions of a four lane blacktop and the roaring of a plane,

He cries in quiet anguish, Great Spirit, feel his pain.

He sees his nation's children fall before the gun,

The ending of an era and yet he does not run.

Here on this lonely hilltop he will make a final stand,

If he dies, he dies in freedom with others of his band.

A moment out of history that all must not forget,

His honor and his virtue lie among us yet.

Steel and Ice

Alone out on the highway in his big old diesel car,
I'm told he is the kind of man that you can't push too far.

They say he is as cold as ice and twice as hard as steel,
But no one ever asks him how he cares or what he feels.

There is one that knows him and he took her as his bride,
Thirty years thereafter and she's still there by his side.

With her he is different and she knows his hopes and fears,
She has seen him smile and watched his eyes well up with tears.

With her he is a different man than the world will ever know,
It's only when he's in her arms that he ever lets it show.

She knows how much he loves though he finds it hard to say,
So he shows his love to her in many other ways.

She watched him touch a newborn child, saw his eyes fill up
with tears,
Felt him tremble as he touched her and knew his love these
many years.

To her it does not matter how others see her man,
She knows that he will love her the very best he can.

He tries to say the many words that a woman wants to hear
She knows that life without her is his greatest fear.

Pixies

When I was just a little child lying in my bed

A little Pixie she would come and sprinkle stardust on my head.

Then the little Pixie off with me would fly,

To visit all our little friends and dance across the sky.

My friend Tigger, he would come and Pooh, that naughty bear

Pixies, Imps and Fairies would dance across the air.

We laughed and played with Dragons, sailed with Pirate Kings

Danced with Queens and Sorcerers inside a Fairy ring.

Then one night she was gone and I knew that I was grown,

You must be a little child to have a Pixie of your own.

Still she can come and visit every once in a while,

Because inside every adult there is still a little child.

The Bend

She walked into the truckstop, looked a little out of place.

It might have been the way she moved or the sad look on her face.

She looked the whole place over, but there wasn't much to see,

Then she walked across the room and sat down across from me.

She asked if I was headed west? I nodded that she was right.

She asked if she could get a ride? I told her that I might.

She said I reminded her of the man that she called Dad.

I got up to pay my bill, said, "Is that good or bad?

She didn't really answer but just gave a little smile,

She never said another word until we'd gone 'bout fifty miles.

She said it was on the curve ahead that her Dad had met his end,

He laid his old Mack over as he went around the bend.

She said, "My Dad's name was Jim and his last name,
it was Beck."

That gave me quite a shock as I'd pulled him from that wreck.

We drove on talking quietly as we thundered through the night.

We talked about my old friend Jim until the sun came into sight.

The Bend (continued)

I told her of her Daddy and the many miles we'd shared,

How much he had talked of her and how very much he'd cared.

I saw a change come over her and she began to cry,

Said she had stopped at the truckstop 'stead of committing suicide.

She had headed out that morning to find a place to die,

Then a little voice inside her head said, "Go for one more ride."

I pulled my old truck to the side and held her in my arms

Told her it was her father's love that had kept her safe from harm.

That happened seven years ago, but she called me yesterday,

Told me all about her three-year-old and the new one on its way.

Said since she had called the first one Jim would it be OK with me,

If this one had my name, the man that helped her see,

That a father's love is forever and death is not an end

Sometimes it takes a leap of faith to make it around the bend.

Fire

The day is dark at noon as smoke rises to the sky.

It takes the heart out of a man to see a forest die.

A fir without a needle, stripped of life-giving bark,

Once so green and vibrant, now so cold and dark.

Land that rang with birdcalls, where squirrels ran to play,

Now silent and so still on this dark and gloomy day.

A stream where deer did drink, where wild ducks raised
their young,

Now choked with ash and cinders and hidden from the sun.

This forest once so full of life now silent dark and dead,

Mother Nature pays the price as the sky glows an eerie red.

Life and Death

Alone out on the highway, I wander through my mind,

Wander back in my dreams to another place and another time.

Huddled around a campfire, I hear a wild wolf call,

I shiver in my cloak of skins, death is on the prowl.

Another fire, another time, sword and armor by my side,

I hear the sound of thundering hooves as death takes
a nighttime ride.

Next is a dark and moonless night and I see by cockpit lights,

A bomber sows its deadly seed, death rides the sky this night.

Then I see him standing there dressed in a cloak of white,

He reaches out and takes my hand and leads me towards the light.

He says, "If you will just believe, my son, then you will never die,

I gave the gift of eternal life to those that will really try.

You need never fear, my son, just place your hand in mine,

We will dwell together until the end of time."

Thoughts of Home

Alone out on the highway, I contemplate my youth,

Though it is hard to do, I must admit the truth.

This life I have chosen and these highways that I roam,

Have given me my freedom, but a truck is not a home.

No sitting in the back yard, listening to my children play,

Or resting on the front porch at the closing of the day.

No working in the garden, planting peas and corn,

Kneeling in the back shed while a kitten is being born.

I'm the one that made the choice, I have no one else to blame,

Still this old truck is not a home. The two just aren't the same.

Stillness

Alone among the forest, stillness fills my mind,

Birds are softly calling to others of their kind.

The silence drapes around me with the gently falling rain,

My inner soul recharges to face the world again.

Snow Geese

Autumn on the prairie and plants have ceased to grow,

Nature seems to hold its breath waiting for the winter's snow.

The mornings now are cooler, there has been a touch of frost,

Birds seem to circle endlessly almost like they are lost.

Suddenly I see them, the whole sky turns to white,

A hundred thousand Snow Geese on their annual southward flight.

They circle over the grain fields, motionless I stand,

Suddenly all around me the geese begin to land.

In just a mere moment the field has turned to white,

Their voices all around me, I am awestruck by the sight.

I stand, barely breathing as they glisten in the sun,

So touched by their beauty, I forget I hold a gun.

Slowly I settle to the ground, like a bird upon a nest.

I sit quietly among them, I cannot disturb their rest.

Later they rise, are gone, heading south towards the sun,

Surrounded by their beauty, I never fired my gun.

Yet they gave me something that no man can describe.

I hear their voices echo and join them on their ride.

Coming Home

I've got them big wheels turning
        I've got that diesel burning
                Home, I'm coming home

Six whole weeks I've been gone
        Baby that's away too long
                Home, I'm coming home

Ten more miles to drive tonight
        Then I get to hold you tight
                Home, I'm coming home

One more turn and I'll be kissing
        Those lips I've been missing
                Home, I'm coming home

Hear my big engine winding down
        My driveway's at the edge of town
                Home, I'm coming home

Slide the key into the lock
        Baby, I've no time to knock
                Home, I'm coming home

Excuse me if I may be staring
        At that towel you're almost wearing
                Home, I'm glad I'm home.

The Younger Generation

This younger generation has me a little worried,

At least before they get in charge I'll probably be buried.

They seem to want so many things and they want them all
right now,

They don't want to work for it, it should just show up somehow.

Everything that I have, from my house to my gray hair,

I got with toil and sweat, but they don't think that's fair.

They depend on the Government, from the cradle to the grave.

That forgot how to work and sweat and how to save.

Governments get larger and I begin to lose my rights,

Maybe it is time for me to stand up and fight.

I don't need no bureaucrat telling me what to do,

Wonder if I start the fight will others join in too.

Unicorns

I wandered to a forest glen with the full moon shining bright.

The world took on a softer glow in its unearthly light.

Silence all around me, then a whisper in the night,

Then I see them in the glen bathed in the soft moonlight,

Hides that shine like silver and horns like purest gold,

A legend somehow come to life, a fable I've been told.

Surrounded by a herd of Unicorns, I watch them leap and play,

Quietly I join with them. Will they let me stay?

Silently in the moonlight we play tag and hide and seek,

Never have I felt so free. I could go on all week.

Then dawn's first ray of sunshine touches where we play,

These creatures of the moonlight vanish with the coming day.

I'll come back another night when the moon is shining bright,

To play again with the Unicorns in the full moon's gentle light.

Until that time, I've memories, my heart and mind are free,

To wander with my childhood friends in the land of make-believe.

Cold Mistress

This highway is a mistress with a heart as cold as steel

She uses and abuses everyone that swings a wheel.

She takes you and claims you, marks you as her own,

She is always with you even when you are at home.

She fills your head with wanderlust, fills your heart with pain

Even when you leave her, she draws you back again.

She is the other woman to which we give our life,

Draws you from your family, your children and your wife.

She takes you and she uses you until you are gray and old,

Then leaves you lying in the ditch, lonely, dead and cold.

Lonely

This highway is a lonely place as I travel across this land,

I need a friend beside me to lend a helping hand.

And then I realize that he's sitting by my side,

He's always been there with me, he comes on every ride.

The thunder of the diesel tells me I am not alone,

His voice is all around me and he'll bring me safely home.

I feel his gentle presence and bask in his boundless love,

The son of God, Jesus Christ, is watching from above.

The Duke and the Duchess

It was a cold and lonely crossroad about three miles out of town,
A heavy rain was falling the night she flagged the Duke down.

She said that she was leaving, that she'd go anywhere,
Wherever he was headed would beat what she had there.

Slowly they began to talk as they rode on through the night,
Talked about their hopes and dreams until the sun came into sight.

She said that she was running from a life of grief and strife,
Running from a man that had beat her since she became his wife.

He talked to her of wandering and a life lived all alone,
He spoke about his loneliness and someone to call his own.

They spoke of disappointments, talked about others' lies,
They began to see each other through the other's eyes.

What they found that night was sent from high above,
While others call it kismet I just call it love.

She found a man much better than the one she left behind,
He found the kind of lady that he'd never dreamed he'd find.

Duke is still out there trucking but there are no more lonely rides,
Now he travels down the road with the Duchess by his side.

That happened twenty years ago and I still wish them
the best of luck,
I remind them every time we meet that good things come by truck.

Dreams

Tenderly I touch you as we lie there in our bed,

Gently you cuddle closer, my arm beneath your head.

Slowly we move together surrounded by the night,

Together we share a love that makes the whole world right.

The clamor of the alarm clock, I awake all alone,

Another lonely truckstop a thousand miles from home.

As I drive away I wonder, do you also dream of me?

When you are alone in bed, do your thoughts run wild and free?

Do we really lie together somewhere up above

Do people share their dreams, could this be part of love?

I'd like to believe that we meet up in the night,

So we can dream together until the morning light.

High Beams

I see him in my mirrors,
           He's coming up real fast.

His bright lights almost blind me,
           I hope that he will pass.

He settles in behind me,
           Like a bird upon a nest.

Does he know about the dimmer switch?
           Could he pass a driving test?

Sixty feet behind me
           Headlights still on bright.

My cab lit up like daylight,
           It's the middle of the night.

I back off to forty,
           It will get him off my rear.

Finally he slides on by,
           Cell phone glued to his ear.

I pick up my speed again,
           Down the road I go.

Way back in my mirror,
           I spot another rosy glow.

Alone

The house was cold and empty when I walked in the door

Then I saw your wedding ring and a note upon the floor.

The note said you were leaving and your ring told me goodbye,

That's when I fell to my knees and I began to cry.

The lifestyle of a trucker and all our time apart,

Had finally got the best of you and left me with a broken heart.

I wandered slowly through the house that once had been our home,

My footsteps echoed down the hall and I knew I was alone.

Then that noisy old alarm clock brought me up wide awake,

I'm in some old parking lot with another run to make.

I stumble across the parking lot to get some coffee, eggs and toast,

My mind wanders back into my dream and what I fear the most.

I fumble for the telephone; I have to make this call.

I pray that you will be at home in our bedroom, down the hall.

I hear your sleepy voice and you sound so sad and blue,

I apologize for waking you just to say that I love you.

No, my dear, there is nothing wrong, just you I had to hear,

I had to say I'm coming home, just to hold you near.

Quiet and Deep

Talk with me, walk with me, touch me with your smile,

Reach out and take my hand, stay with me for a while.

Show me that you love me, tell me with your eyes,

Let me know you missed me, tell me with your sighs.

Hold me while we're sleeping, warm me with your touch.

Let me be in your dreams, your love means so very much.

Smile at me while I am leaving, please try not to weep,

You know my love for you is true, it's quiet but it's deep.

My memories are made of you and I replay them while I'm gone,

You know I will be coming home, I won't stay away too long.

Two Lives – One Highway

She's cleaning up the house today, home there all alone.
Her children are at school, her husband is far from home.

He's out there on the highway trying to make a buck,
Running coast to coast in a big old diesel truck.

Many times she's wondered, could he not work nine to five?
It's only when he's at home that she really feels alive.

He's out there on the road and has one more drop to make,
Then he'll hit the truckstop, have a shower, take a break,

He'll figure out his schedule then he'll call her there at home.
There are times that he feels guilty, leaving her alone.

Still he makes a living and keeps the food upon the table,
He wishes he could be home more, would be if he was able.

Two very different courses on the long highway of life,
Still they work together as a husband and a wife.

They have their time together at the ending of each run,
That's when they relax and have some family fun.

Both take these special times and keep them in their heart,
Memories of better times when they are far apart.

The lifestyle of a trucker is unlike any other
With love and faith and a little luck they keep it all together.

Steelhead

I'm knee deep in a rushing stream beneath a clear blue sky,

Suddenly, with a mighty swirl, a fish rises to my fly.

My rod takes on an arc and the reel begins to scream,

Slowly and carefully I follow him downstream.

He fights in the deep water where he has room to run,

Then with a mighty leap, he glistens in the sun.

A silver fish with a bright red stripe dives back in the water,

A mighty Northern steelhead, a fighter like no other.

Slowly I regain some line, my wrists begin to ache,

My rod bends almost double, how much will it take?

Now the fish begins to tire and I lead him towards the land,

Gently now I use my net and now hold him in my hands.

Slowly, with trembling hands, I reach and remove the fly,

I will return him to the stream; he does not deserve to die.

Quietly he lies there, we both need time to breathe,

A flick of his tail and he is gone, now I turn to leave.

I turn back again and see him swirl as he returns to the deep,

He will live to fight again, it's his memory I keep.

Over Yonder

Why was I born to wander, to always be alone?

Not to be like other men who settle down at home?

Did a freight train's lonely whistle touch me as a child?

Could it have been the restless wind or a wolf howl from the wild?

Are there greener pastures somewhere around some bend?

Could there be only traveling on a road that has no end?

Still I travel onward, I guess I was born to wander,

The place that I am looking for is somewhere over yonder.

Hummingbirds

Ever watch a Hummingbird as it rests after flight?

Their feathers shine iridescent in the bright sunlight.

They have perched upon my finger; I've cupped them in my hand,

First you have to earn their trust before they choose to land.

So much like a little child, their love you also earn,

Trust is not an inborn thing; It's something we must learn.

Memories

Some things last just seconds. I remember our first kiss.

Other last fleeting moments, holding you is bliss.

Some things last for years and we leave them with regret

Memories last forever, and I will not forget.

Times we walked together by the river hand in hand,

Remember the beach, walking barefoot in the sand?

The times we spent together I remember with a smile,

They sustain me on the highway across many a lonely mile.

I'm driving down the highway, traveling coast to coast,

The time we spent together is what I remember most.

Some things last for seconds and we leave them with regret,

My memories will last forever, never will I forget.

Eastbound

He loaded up and rolled away eastbound through the night,
His big old diesel running hard and the headlights burning bright.

Hauling lumber from the coast on the big road all alone,
He rolled over in Montana and he's never coming home.

They said there was a camper van broke down on the road,
When he swerved to miss them he rolled his heavy load.

Her man won't be coming home; he's taken his last ride,
Forty tons of steel and wood rolled over on its side.

They said with his dying breath as they took him from the road
He said he loved his lady and he cursed the damned old road.

She never got to tell him about the new life that had begun,
He died there in Montana not knowing about his son.

That child now stands beside her, grown to be a man,
He says the road is calling him to be the best he can.

Oh Lord, please protect him when he's out there on that road,
Montana is a driver and he pulls those heavy loads.

Now he's loaded up and rolling eastbound in the night,
A big old diesel running hard, headlights burning bright.

Two Lonely People

She sits there in that darkened bar and slowly sips her wine,

Wanders in her memories to another place, another time

Memories of a faded past and a love that seemed so right,

These memories reach out for her on cold and lonely nights.

A stranger walks into the bar, sits down and buys a beer,

She wonders who he is and what he is doing here?

He reminds her of so many men and so many wasted nights,

Looking for the special one to help to make things right.

Slowly he looks around and he checks out every face,

He is another searcher in this dark and lonely place.

As he looks around the bar, his mind begins to wander,

Memories of a long-lost love somewhere way back yonder.

Just two lost and lonely people living in the past,

Remembering how it used to be, searching for something to last.

Will they try to find themselves in each other's arms tonight?

Will this keep the tears away until the morning light?

They sit there on their bar stools, she slowly sips her wine,

He has another drink of beer, both lost in the whirl of time.

The Highway

This highway reaches out for me, touches my inner soul

This mistress of destiny tells me to let it roll.

She tells of greener pastures as I thunder through the night,

Always over another hill maybe to the left or right.

What is this hold she has on me, why do I heed her song?

She's a taker, not a giver, and this road is oh, so long.

Why was I born to wander, to look over another hill,

To listen to Coyote's howl and hear the Whippoorwill?

The lonesome call of an air horn, the tires how they cry,

The thunder of a diesel as it goes flying by.

Why do I heed this lonesome call, listen to this song?

This cold and lonely highway keeps me moving ever on.

Prairie Storm

A storm upon the prairies, clouds go rolling by,

Rain bounces off the pavement beneath a darkened sky.

Lightning flashes nearby and I hear the thunder roll,

Words cannot do it justice as it fills my very soul.

Hailstones pound across the land, my wipers beat in vain,

The sky seems to burst asunder as the lightning strikes again.

In moments there is silence and again the sun can shine.

The summer storm has moved along somewhere else
down the line.

The Trucker

He's a driver, a mechanic, an executive in jeans,

He's a long haul driver and he knows what freedom means.

Freedom is a highway and a decent paying load,

Freedom is a way of life and an ever-changing road.

Yet for this kind of freedom there is a price to pay,

It seems he is away from home forever and a day.

He missed his family growing up, their troubles and their fears,

Many times, by telephone he has listened to their tears.

The baseball, the ballet, the birthdays and that dance,

He wanted to be there for them but never had a chance.

There was always one more load, but it kept his family fed,

His work brings home the bacon and keeps them warm in bed.

Just one more load then he'll go home, but he can't stay too long,

He's addicted to the highway and the diesel's heavy song.

My Campsite

A full moon rides across the sky and throws its reflection
on the lake.

I hear the sound of a lonesome Loon calling for its mate.

An Owl drifts by on soundless wings, searching for a meal,

A Raccoon slips along the shore, looking for some food to steal.

The tall pines whisper softly, stirred by a gentle breeze,

It curls around my campsite and rustles the Aspen leaves.

My campfire dies to embers as I sit here on this log,

I hear the sound of Bullfrogs calling from a peaty bog.

The stars shine in the heavens like candles in the sky,

The moon now hides its glory as a puffy cloud sails by.

The hustle of my city life slowly fades away,

I close my eyes and drift away into another day.

Baby, Child, and Man.

Rockets fell upon the city,

    a newborn baby cried.

New life came to England,

    around him others died.

Soon a ship to Canada

    a place he would call home.

Raised on a working farm,

    room for a child to roam.

A little one-room schoolhouse,

    a church among the trees.

He grew to be a young man,

    running wild and free.

Raised by a loving family,

    knowing right from wrong.

Taught love of God and country,

    this helped to make him strong.

Baby, Child, and Man (continued)

Grown, now he joined the service,

    there he learned how to fight.

Then trips to many foreign lands,

    he did what he thought was right.

Next a return to Canada,

    shunned for what he had done.

He started driving big rigs,

    found peace on the endless runs.

A chance meeting with a lady,

    she soon became his wife.

Children followed later,

    the start of his new life.

Still he drove the big trucks,

    across the endless land.

North and south, east and west,

    guided by his steady hand.

Somehow he kept his family fed,

Baby, Child, and Man (continued)

taught his children wrong and right.

Now in his later years,

he takes the time to write.

Tales of where he wandered,

people he has known.

The family that he cares for,

this land that he calls home.

Somehow he must make a mark,

pass on the lesson he has learned.

Freedom is not given,

it's something that you earn.

Dave Madill

CPSIA information can be obtained at www.ICGtesting.com
Printed in the USA
LVOW10s1505031113

359812LV00001B/104/P